ACET fb BOOKS

were ancient heresies disguised social movements?

A. H. M. JONES

HISTORICAL SERIES

S0-BYT-045

FACET BOOKS

HISTORICAL SERIES

FACET fb BOOKS

HISTORICAL SERIES — 1

Clarence L. Lee, Editor

Were Ancient Heresies

Disguised Social Movements?

by A. H. M. JONES

FORTRESS PRESS   PHILADELPHIA

This study appeared originally under the title
"Were Ancient Heresies National or Social Movements in Disguise?"
in *The Journal of Theological Studies*, New Series,
Vol. X, Part 2 (1959), pp. 280-297
(published by Oxford University Press, London).

Published by Fortress Press, 1966
INTRODUCTION © 1966 BY FORTRESS PRESS
Library of Congress Catalog Card Number 66-11534

2711H65   Printed in U.S.A.   UB3023

Introduction

HERESY and schism are by no means the simple phenomena which they have often been purported to be by historians and students alike. The so-called "classical" theory of the origin of heresy, for instance, presupposed that heresies were mere perversions brought about by vain curiosity and the inordinate pride of their originators. According to this view (which, unfortunately, has dominated the church's attitude toward heresy throughout most of its history) all deviations from the truth can be accounted for in terms of the wickedness and shortcomings of the heretics themselves.

From a critical point of view, the classical theory's assumption that heresy is nothing more than the voiced opinion of vain and prideful men is much too facile. Historical scholarship has demonstrated that behind every heresy and schismatic movement in the history of the church there are factors much more complex and subtle than the personality flaws of the leaders of such movements. The personal factor—pride, ambition, jealousy—may indeed be cited as the immediate occasion for the appearance of many heresies and schisms, but even in such instances it is possible to find other forces and issues of more profound significance.

When examined from a theological perspective, the

diverse origins of heretical-schismatic movements become immediately apparent. Some heresies, as H. E. W. Turner[1] has shown in his study of the relationship between heterodoxy and orthodoxy in the early church, resulted from the attempt to accommodate the teachings of the church to the prevailing thought forms and cultural values of the society in which Christianity found itself. Such accommodations, exemplified chiefly by gnosticism, led to what Turner calls the dilution of the gospel. The essentially "liberal" theological attitude which motivated this type of heretical development is clearly different from the reactionary instincts which motivated many of the schismatic groups in the early church. Here, instead of the gospel's being diluted by foreign elements, the teachings of the church were distorted by a conservatism which denied Christianity the right to exploit meaningfully the culture and philosophy of the civilizations to which it addressed itself. An examination of other heresies and schismatic movements would reveal an even greater diversity of origins in terms of theological motivation.

Perhaps even more important than a recognition of the extremely complicated theological background against which the study of heresy and schism must be made, however, is a recognition of the various non-theological factors which may have contributed to the rise of disruptive movements in the church. This aspect of the study of heresy and schism was one seldom taken into account in the past, particularly when deal-

[1] H. E. W. Turner, *The Pattern of Christian Truth* (London: Mowbray, 1954).

ing with the heresies and schisms of the early church. Most scholars recognized that external factors of political and economic nature played a significant role in the upheaval in the life and thought of the church in the sixteenth century. Few, however, were alert to the possibility that the very same factors were equally at work in the heresies and schisms of the early church. Usually, such great controversies of the early church as the Donatist schism of the fourth century or the christological controversy of the fifth century were treated as completely self-contained theological disputes which involved nothing more than the doctrinal issues themselves. In keeping with the classical theory concerning the origin of heresies and schisms, scholars continued to portray the leaders of such movements as obdurate, selfish perverters of the truth. This uncritical portrayal of the personal element, however, did not detract from the almost exclusive preoccupation with the doctrinal issues of the controversies.

It was this very concentration on the doctrinal aspects of the disputes in the early church which eventually prompted scholars to look behind the often highly abstruse theological issues for other, non-theological factors which might more easily explain not only the appearance but also the persistence of the early heresies and schisms. Is it possible, these scholars asked themselves, that something as recondite as the relationship between the two natures of Christ could serve as the basis upon which a large segment of the Christian population in the East would separate itself from the so-called orthodox church? Is it possible that something as ambiguous as the moral credentials of the clergy could serve as the basis for a major schism in the West?

Questions such as these gave rise to efforts to uncover mundane factors as motivating forces of heresy and schism in the early church. These efforts are well-known to the specialists in church history, but perhaps less well-known to the non-specialist. A wide variety of these mundane factors has been suggested. In the christological controversy, for instance, a clash over jurisdictional rights between the two most powerful ecclesiastics in the East, the bishops of Alexandria and Constantinople, seems to have contributed both to the rise as well as to the continuation of the dispute. As the controversy has been seen by many scholars, the bitter, and, at times, fanatical theological argumentation which it engendered might never have arisen at all had it not been for the element of ecclesiastical rivalry which prompted the disputants to employ theological issues as convenient pretexts for attacking their most threatening competition.

Another interpretation of the same controversy finds semantic difficulties[2] at the basis of the dispute. The inability of theologians to communicate with each other due to language problems has, in fact, been a frequent cause of misunderstanding in the church. Coupled with other disruptive factors, such as ecclesiastical rivalry, these semantic difficulties have been pointed to as contributing to the rise of schismatic movements in the church.

[2] Cf. R. V. Sellers, *Two Ancient Christologies* (London: S.P.C.K., 1954).

By far the most important and provocative of the factors which have been suggested as contributory factors to heresy and schism in the early church, however, are those which involve the political and social aspirations of the people who embraced the various heresies and schisms. According to this line of investigation, the problems faced by large segments of the population in the Roman Empire were strikingly similar to the problems faced by masses of people today. There was, for example, the problem of colonialism or imperialism. Certain sections of the empire were beginning to develop a consciousness of national or regional identity, and thus were eager to throw off the yoke of Roman imperialism. Since orthodox Christianity was supposedly identified with the Roman imperium in such sections, it has been claimed that the heteredox or schismatic movements which arose there must be viewed, in part, at least, as a means of registering nationalistic protest.

Another problem, equally modern in ring, was that of the class struggle between the peasantry and the aristocracy of the empire. In this struggle, the lower classes supposedly regarded the orthodox or catholic church as the creature of the ruling aristocracy, and hence tended to use heretical-schismatic movements as outlets for expressing their social and economic discontent.

For the modern student, such estimates of the background of early Christian heresy and schism cannot help but be provocative. Instead of being seen as mere quarrels over theological trivialities, the internal disputes in the early church can be interpreted as having involved issues of obvious contemporary relevance. It is precisely at this point, however, that caution must be enjoined lest the facts of history be overridden by a concern for contemporaneity. While it may be assumed that heresy and schism are much more problematic than the classical theory concerning their origins suggests, it is nevertheless questionable whether the problems of today can be used to illuminate the causes and character of these early Christian movements.

This, essentially, is the position taken by A. H. M. Jones in the following study. Jones believes that contemporary scholarship has been too eager to discover modern forces and ideals at work in such ancient heresies and schisms as Arianism, Donatism, and Monophysitism. The mere fact that these sects happened to coincide with certain social or regional groups, he claims, does not necessarily mean that they were national or social movements in disguise. After a careful examination of the historical evidence, Jones concludes that these ancient heresies and schisms, complex as they may have been, did not conceal any political or social goals beneath their theological-ecclesiastical dissent.

Jones's study, therefore, is a necessary corrective to the position which has come to be so widely advocated in recent studies of heresy and schism in the early church. Perhaps more important than its effective challenging of the thesis that ulterior motives of a political or social character underlie the major ancient heresies and schisms, however, is its equally effective demonstration that the most basic motivation behind every heresy and schism is the conviction on the part of the heretics and schismatics that they are right and their opponents wrong. This simple point is frequently overlooked in the altogether justifiable and necessary search for the many subtle forces and non-theological factors which have contributed to the rise and persistence of heresy and schism. From a historical point of view, the interpretation which sees heresy and schism as having involved nothing more than various deviations from the established theological norms of the church is clearly unsatisfactory; but so, also, is the interpretation which fails to recognize that these deviations, no matter how trivial and, at times, irrational, nevertheless represented the genuine convictions of those who held them.

Arnold Hugh Martin Jones received his education in Great Britain's Cheltenham College and New College, Oxford. After participating in the excavation of Constantinople and Jerash (1927-1929), he was a reader in ancient history at the Egyptian University in Cairo. From 1939 to 1946 he was a lecturer in ancient history at Wadham College and served with the military intelligence. From 1946 to 1951 he was professor of ancient history at University College, London, and since 1951 he has been professor of ancient history at Cambridge University and a fellow of Jesus College.

CLARENCE L. LEE

Lutheran Theological Seminary
Philadelphia, Pennsylvania
Spring, 1966

WERE ANCIENT HERESIES
DISGUISED SOCIAL MOVEMENTS?

MOST modern historians of the later Roman Empire, whether secular or ecclesiastical, seem to agree
that certain of the heresies and schisms of that period
were in some sense national rather than purely religious
movements.[1] They point to the fact that some heresies
either were confined to certain areas, as was Donatism
to Africa, or were at any rate particularly strong and
persistent in some districts or among some peoples, as
were Monophysitism in Egypt and Syria, or Arianism
among the German tribes. They stress the fact that
among these groups indigenous languages—Punic or
Berber in Africa, Coptic, Syriac, or German—were
adopted by the heretical or schismatic churches. Their

[1] For a thoroughgoing statement of this thesis see E. L. Woodward,
Christianity and Nationalism in the Later Roman Empire (London:
Longmans, Green and Co., 1916). The latest great historian of the
period, Ernst Stein, *Geschichte des spätrömischen Reiches* (Vienna,
1928), I; *Histoire du Bas-Empire* (Paris, 1949), II, is its strong
advocate. It is also adopted by the authors of *De la paix Con-
stantinienne à la mort de Théodose* (J. R. Palanque, G. Bardy, P. de
Labriolle, Paris, 1945), and *De la mort de Théodose à l'élection de
Grégoire le Grand* (P. de Labriolle, G. Bardy, L. Bréhier, G. de
Plinval, Paris, 1947), Vols. III and IV of *Histoire de l'eglise*, ed.
A. Fliche and V. Martin.

general line of argument is that mere doctrinal differences, often of extreme subtlety, could not have engendered such powerful and enduring movements, and that their real and underlying cause must be sought in national sentiment. They often maintain that under the later Roman Empire long-dormant nationalism arose or revived in a number of areas, and was an important contributory cause in the downfall of the empire; for the dissident groups not merely stubbornly resisted the efforts of the imperial government to impose religious conformity upon them, but struggled to break away from the empire, supporting local pretenders or foreign invaders.

At the risk of a certain crudity I should like to state this thesis in more concrete terms. Did the average Copt say to himself, "I am an Egyptian and proud of it. I hate the Roman oppressor, and will at the earliest opportunity cast off the alien yoke. Meanwhile I insist on speaking my native Coptic instead of Greek, the language of the foreign government, and I refuse to belong to its church. I do not know or care whether Christ has one or two natures, but as the Romans insist on the latter view, I hold the former"? This statement of the case appears to be implied by some historians, who speak of the heresies as a mere screen for nationalist aspirations. But if the last sentence seems to be too cynical even for the most private thoughts, one might substitute for it, "The Romans anyhow are heretics; we Egyptians are clearly right in believing that Christ has one nature only. I will firmly reject any compromise which the Romans may offer, and even if they accept our view I will never be reconciled with them." [2]

If they felt like this the heretics fairly certainly did not put their sentiments into writing. We are not, it is true, so well provided with heretical literature as we could wish: if the German Arians wrote anything, it has been lost. But we possess a considerable bulk of Monophysite literature, including theological treatises, letters, and histories both ecclesiastical and secular. Some Donatist writings have been preserved, and others can be reconstructed from Augustine's elaborate refutations of them. In the vast amount of controversial literature on the orthodox side some references would surely be found to the nationalist sentiments of their opponents if they had voiced them openly. What the sectaries actually said in public, so far as our record goes, was—to change the instance—"The Donatist church is the true Catholic church, and we will never communicate with traditores," but what they thought, we are asked to believe, was: "We are Africans and hate the Rome government; we will have nothing to do with the Romans and will maintain our African church and if possible set up our African state."

This is a thesis which is obviously difficult to prove or to disprove, for one cannot easily read the secret thoughts of men who lived fifteen hundred years ago. One can only examine their written words with care, in case they have inadvertently revealed their real thoughts, or endeavor to deduce their thoughts from their actions and policies.

---

[2] The last clause is required by Stein's view; see below, p. 15.

It could also be held that the sectaries not only said, but in their conscious thought believed, that their quarrel with the government was purely religious, but that they really held their peculiar views because they were in harmony with their national temperament or were emotionally linked with their national group, and conversely really hated the orthodox because they were foreigners, though they genuinely thought that they condemned them as heretics. On this hypothesis the conscious thought of a Copt might be: "We Egyptians are right in believing that Christ has one nature, and I abominate the Romans as heretics and hate them as persecutors. Rather than submit to their rule I would welcome a barbarian invader." Or he might even say no more than: "We hold the true orthodox faith, and I abominate the government because it is heretical and persecutes us," but really hate the Romans as foreigners.

In this attenuated form the nationalist hypothesis is even more difficult to prove or disprove. One can seek to discover whether hostility to the Roman government persisted even when it accepted the theological view of the dissident groups. One can inquire whether the theological views of the sectaries show any affinity with the pre-Christian beliefs of the group which held them. One can finally inquire how far adherence to certain theological views was coterminous with national groups, defined by criteria of language or religion.

To turn from generalities to special cases I will first consider the Donatists. Donatism was confined to the African provinces, and within that area it was both widespread and persistent, at all times commanding a wide following and at some periods dominating the whole country, and surviving despite many persecutions for almost three centuries to our certain knowledge, and probably longer. Many, if not most, of its adherents were Punic- or Berber-speaking, and its greatest strength lay in the least Romanized areas, especially southern Numidia. In some of its beliefs and practices, in particular in its morbid emphasis on martyrdom, it seems to show affinities with the pagan religion of the area. Its leaders cooperated with two native pretenders, Firmus and Gildo, and some of them are alleged to have had treasonable dealings with certain Goths in the early fifth century.[3]

To take their political activities first, the Donatists were certainly not anti-imperial at the beginning: they in fact appealed to the emperor against the Caecilianists.[4] When Constantine had finally rejected their cause, they raised the cry that the state should not interfere in religion[5]—as later the Homoousian party did when Constantius II favored the Arians.[6] But when Julian ordered the restoration of banished clergy and confiscated church property they were happy to accept imperial aid.[7] That they cooperated with Firmus[8] and

[3] The evidence for these statements is well stated in W. H. C. Frend's work, *The Donatist Church* (Oxford: Clarendon, 1952), from which I differ only in some points of emphasis and interpretation.

[4] Augustine *Epistula* 88; Optatus *De schismate Donatistarum adversus Parmenianum* i. 22.

[5] Optatus, *op. cit.*, iii. 3, *"quid imperatori cum ecclesia?"*

[6] Hilary, *Liber I ad Constantium.*

[7] Optatus, *op. cit.*, ii. 16; Augustine *Contra Litteras Petiliani* ii. 97. 224.

[8] Augustine *Epistula* 87. 10; *Contra Epistulam Parmeniani* i. 10. 16, 11. 17; *Contra Litteras Petiliani* ii. 83.

Gildo[9] need mean no more than that the pretenders exploited local grievances to win support for their personal ambitions, and that the Donatists, who by now had little hope of obtaining what they wanted from the legitimate government, decided to risk backing a pretender who might be successful. With a good deal less excuse the Spanish bishop Ithacius, when Gratian, or rather his master of the offices, supported the Priscillianists, transferred his allegiance to the usurper Maximus;[10] and yet no one has suggested that the Catholic Ithacius was a Spanish nationalist. It may be claimed that Firmus and Gildo, unlike Maximus, were leaders of national rebellions, but beyond the fact that they came from a Moorish princely family, there is nothing to suggest that they were not usurpers of the normal type, that is, ambitious individuals seeking for personal power. The record of the members of the family certainly does not suggest zeal for any cause but their own. When Firmus rebelled, his brother Gildo took the Roman side, and received the promotion on which he had no doubt counted. When he in turn rebelled, another brother, Mascazel, led the army which crushed him. There is in fact no reason to believe that the rebellions of Firmus and Gildo were different in kind from that of Alexander the Phrygian before them, or those of Heraclian and Boniface after them.

The negotiations of the Donatists with the Goths are only known from a letter of Augustine to Count Boniface, who had inquired whether Donatism and Arianism

---

[9] Frend, *op. cit.*, pp. 208 ff.
[10] Sulpicius Severus *Chronicle* ii. 48-49.

had any points in common.[11] Augustine replied that they had none, but that "sometimes, as we have heard, some of them, wishing to conciliate the Goths to themselves, because they see that they have some power, say that they have the same beliefs as they." It seems very unlikely that the Donatists were in touch with the Visigoths settled in Aquitania, and Boniface's interest in the matter suggests that it was his Gothic federates who were approached. If so, the Donatists were merely making propaganda among influential persons in the entourage of the Comes Africae, and perhaps trying to curry favor with the Comes himself, who, we learn from a later letter of Augustine,[12] married an Arian wife. Or was Boniface himself thinking of striking an alliance with the Donatists when he put his question to Augustine? Augustine answers the question with the utmost brevity, and goes on to expatiate for pages on the doctrinal and historical issues involved. It is hard to believe that if he had had any suspicion that the Donatists were plotting treason against the empire he would have dismissed the matter so lightly.

There is no evidence that the Donatists made common cause with the Vandals. All that Victor Vitensis can say against them is that one Donatist, Nicesius, was perverted to Arianism.[13] It is scarcely credible that if they had taken the Vandal side or even secured toleration from them, this would not have been trumpeted abroad by their persecuted Catholic adversaries.

[11] Augustine *Epistula* 185. 1.
[12] Augustine *Epistula* 220. 4.
[13] Victor Vitensis *Historia persecutionis Africanae provinciae* iii. 71.

There is in fact very little hint that the Donatists cherished dreams of a national African state. How far was the movement, in any national sense, African in character? It is no doubt true that a large proportion of Donatists were Punic- or Berber-speaking, and that the Donatist clergy used the indigenous languages for instruction and exhortation. But since Africa was a predominantly rural country, and most rural Africans knew no Latin, it was inevitable that any church which wished to rally the mass of the population had to use the native languages. On the Catholic side Augustine too was anxious to secure Punic-speaking clergy to take charge of rural areas.[14]

Nor was Donatism by any means confined to the humble strata of society where the native languages were spoken. The leaders and apologists of the movement, men like Parmenian (who was not even an African),[15] the learned and eloquent Tyconius,[16] the lawyer Petilian,[17] came from the cultivated and Romanized classes, and the penal law of 412 specifies appropriate penalties not only for circumcellions and plebeians, *negotiatores* and ordinary decurions, but for the higher urban aristocracy, the *principales* and *sacerdotales*, and for senators, *clarissimi*, *spectabiles*, and even *illustres*, the cream of Roman imperial society.[18] There is, furthermore, no suggestion that the Donatists took any

[14] Augustine *Epistula* 84; 209. 3.

[15] Optatus, *op. cit.*, i. 5; ii. 7.

[16] Gennadius *De Viris illustribus* 18; Augustine *Contra Epistulam Parmeniani* i. 1. 1.

[17] Augustine *Contra Litteras Petiliani* iii. 16. 19.

[18] *Codex Theodosianus* XVI. v. 52; cp. 54.

pride in the indigenous languages. Their literature, or what survives of it, was all written in Latin, not only the controversial or apologetic treatises which were aimed at Catholics, but popular works, such as the *Acts of Martyrs*, meant for the encouragement of the faithful. The inscriptions of Donatist churches are all in Latin, even the slogans and war cries of the circumcellions, like the famous "Deo Laudes," were in Latin.

That Donatism may in the course of time have acquired certain African characteristics, derived from the pre-Christian beliefs of the people, may well be true. Popular Christianity everywhere tended to absorb local beliefs and customs. But I wonder whether the Donatist fixation on martyrdom may not be due as much to their quarrel with the Catholics as to any survival of primitive pagan ideas. They claimed to be the church of the martyrs as against the Catholics who were traditores, and martyrdom was therefore to them the touchstone of the true faith.

The Donatists certainly believed that in Africa only did the Catholic church survive, but they seem to have felt somewhat uneasy at their isolation. They apparently made abortive efforts to spread their faith in Spain. They may have negotiated with the Arians of Sardica in the hope of finding churches unsullied by *traditio* in the East. It is significant that the Donatists maintained their own pope in Rome throughout the fourth and early fifth centuries.[19] The fact, however, remained that for all practical purposes their church was confined to Africa, and they were reduced to inter-

[19] Frend, *op. cit.*, pp. 164, 170.

preting a phrase from the Song of Songs, "ubi pascis ubi cubas in meridie," [20] as a prophecy that such was God's will.[21]

That Donatism should have had so strong a hold throughout Africa and should have been confined to Africa can be explained by the historical circumstances in which the movement arose. It would appear that the African provinces were exceptional in that Christianity had already in the latter part of the third century captured the countryside.[22] They were also exceptional in the number of their confessors and martyrs in the Great Persecution [under Diocletian]. These two facts are not unconnected. It is clear from contemporary accounts that in both the Decian and Diocletianic persecutions upper-class Christians lapsed in very large numbers, and that the confessors and martyrs were mainly men and women of the lower orders. This was not unnatural. The upper classes feared for their property and position and could be more easily intimidated by the threat of torture, from which they were normally immune. The poor had less to lose and to them flogging was an everyday occurrence. It may be added that the poor might well hope to pass undetected if they failed to comply with the law, whereas the rich would be more likely to be denounced.

It would seem likely, then, that in Africa a larger proportion of Christians remained steadfast than in most

[20] Song of Songs 1:7: ". . . where you pasture your flock, where you make it lie down at noon."
[21] Augustine *Epistula ad Catholicos* 16. 40; *Sermo* 46. 36-37; 138. 9-10.
[22] Frend, *op. cit.*, pp. 83 ff.

parts of the empire. Not unnaturally they took a less charitable view of the lapsed than that which prevailed in other provinces. Throughout Africa feelings were tense, and a rupture was likely between the rigorist and the lenient groups. The dispute over the election of Caecilian fired the spark, and inevitably involved all Africa, for Carthage had for long been acknowledged as the primatial see of all the African provinces. But outside Africa the churches had no sympathy with the rigorist party, and having decided that Caecilian was the lawful bishop of Carthage they took no further interest in the affair.

Only in one other province do we hear of a similar movement. In Egypt, where as in Africa Christianity had in the third century spread to the rural areas, the resistance to the Diocletianic persecution was stubborn, and a rigorist party, the Melitians, refused to readmit the lapsed to communion.[23] But the Donatists seem never to have made contact with the Melitians; they were too far away. Melitianism remained confined to Egypt, where it lasted into the eighth century at least.[24] But it never became a dominant force there. The claim of the Melitians to be the Church of the Martyrs must have been gravely shaken when Peter of Alexandria, whose lenient views they denounced, himself died as a martyr, and the see of Alexandria was filled by a succession of able and ruthless bishops, who quickly broke the spirit of the rebels.

[23] Frend, *op. cit.*, p. 86. For a full account of the Melitians see H. I. Bell, *Jews and Christians in Egypt* (London: Oxford University Press, 1924), pp. 38 ff.
[24] Bell, *op. cit.*, pp. 42-43.

That Donatism survived so stubbornly is hardly a matter for surprise. Throughout history religious feuds have been long-lived, and have often survived when the original cause of quarrel has been almost forgotten. The Donatists were from the beginning a large group, which it was difficult to stamp out, and the intermittent and not very efficient persecutions which they suffered served only to embitter them—in these circumstances the blood of the martyrs was the seed of the church.

The Copts have a priori a stronger case to be regarded as a nation than the Africans for, whereas the inhabitants of the diocese of Africa had never formed a political unit, Egypt had in the past been a national kingdom, and long after that kingdom had fallen had cherished a strong national sentiment based on the traditions of the past and fostered by its peculiar religion. Under the later Ptolemies there had been revolts which had aimed at expelling the aliens and setting up a native dynasty, and as late as the third century A.D. copies were circulating of the *Prophecy of the Potter*, which holds out apocalyptic hopes of a king who should deliver Egypt from the yoke of the foreigners, and destroy "the city beside the sea" which was "the nurse of all men; every race of men dwelt within her."[25] Alexandria also had its patriotic anti-Roman tradition witnessed by the *Acts of the Pagan Martyrs*, in which the city is represented as the champion of Hellenism against Roman tyrants and their Jewish protégés.[26] The

[25] W. Wilcken, *Hermes*, XL (1905), 544 ff.
[26] Collected in H. A. Musurillo, *The Acts of the Pagan Martyrs* (Oxford: Clarendon, 1954).

anti-Roman movements of Egypt and Alexandria were, it may be noted, quite distinct and mutually hostile; the Alexandrian documents refer with contempt to Egyptians, and the Egyptians reflect hatred of Alexandria.

There is no evidence that either tradition survived the triumph of Christianity. The Egyptian tradition was closely linked with old native religion, and the Alexandrian with pagan Hellenism. Certainly in Christian Egypt no trace survived of the old antagonism between Egypt and Alexandria; Alexandria was the undisputed religious capital of Egypt. This fact seems decisive proof that there was no conscious survival of the old Egyptian nationalism in the Christian period.

The nationalist thesis in the case of Egypt is based on much the same arguments as in that of Africa.[27] It is argued that the stubborn and unanimous devotion of the Egyptians to the Monophysite doctrine must have been derived from some other cause than the very subtle theological issues involved, and was in fact an expression of national Egyptian sentiment and hatred of the Roman Empire. In support of this hypothesis two pieces of evidence are produced, the use of the Coptic language by the Egyptian church, and the alleged welcome given by the Monophysite Egyptians to the Persians and to the Arabs.

[27] For scholarly and moderate statements of the case see J. Maspero, *Histoire des patriarches d'Alexandrie depuis la mort de l'empéreur Anastase jusqu'à la réconciliation des églises jacobites, 518-616* (Paris, 1923); E. R. Hardy, "The Patriarchate of Alexandria: A Study in National Christianity," *Church History*, XV (1946), 81-100; *idem*, *Christian Egypt: Church and People* (New York: Oxford University Press, 1952).

The linguistic point is not convincing. Coptic was the normal language of the great majority of rural Egyptians, very many of whom knew no Greek. It was naturally adopted by the church as soon as Christianity spread to the countryside, and was employed long before the Egyptian church became heretical. Long after the split the intellectual leaders of the Monophysite church continued to be Greek-speaking, and the literature of the movement was written in Greek. Ultimately, it is true, the Monophysite church became purely Coptic and the Orthodox purely Greek; but this was only after the Arab conquest, when Greek gradually died out in Egypt and the native church naturally abandoned its use, while on the other hand the Orthodox patriarch was a nominee of the Byzantine government, often non-resident.

In the sixth century there is no very convincing evidence that Greek-speaking Egyptians favored Chalcedon and Copts opposed it. Alexandria, where the Greek element was strongest, was a stronghold of Monophysitism: John the Almoner, when he became patriarch in the early seventh century, found only seven churches in the hands of Chalcedonians.[28] It may well be that in periods when the penal laws were enforced, members of the local aristocracy conformed for prudential reasons. Flavius Apion was persuaded by "the most pious and faithful emperors," Justin and Justinian, to adopt the Chalcedonian faith: if he had not he might well have forfeited his patrician rank and his great estates. But until the change of emperors made a change

[28] Sophronius *Vita Iohannis Eleemosynarii* 5.

of faith expedient, Flavius Apion, great aristocrat though he was, had been a Monophysite,[29] and his descendants later returned to that faith.[30]

There is no hint of any anti-imperial movement, much less any rebellion, during the period of almost two centuries that elapsed between the Council of Chalcedon and the Arab conquest. The Alexandrians, of course, frequently rioted when the imperial government forced Chalcedonian patriarchs upon them, and considerable bodies of troops had to be used to suppress them. But during the periods when the emperors favored or tolerated Monophysitism, the Egyptians seem to have been content. Ernst Stein has made much of one incident.[31] When in 516 Anastasius, whose Monophysite sympathies were by now quite undisguised, appointed Dioscorus II to succeed John III as patriarch of Alexandria, the people objected that he had been uncanonically installed by the secular authorities, and insisted on the clergy, who had acquiesced, going through the form of electing him again. Next day they lynched the Augustal prefect, for praising Anastasius, according to Theophanes; Malalas says that it was a food shortage that provoked the attack on the Augustal.[32] This incident, Stein argues, proves that the Egyptians

[29] *Acta Conciliorum Oecumenicorum* (Ed., Eduard Schwartz; Berlin, 1933), IV. ii. 170.

[30] J. B. Chabot, *Chronique de Michel le Syrien* (1899), II, 385 (read "Strategios the patrician").

[31] Stein, *op. cit.*, II, 164.

[32] Theophanes, A. M., 6009 (C. de Boor, *Theophanis Chronographia* (Leipzig, 1883); Johannes Malalas, *Chronographia* (Bonn Edition, 1831), p. 401; C. de Boor, *Excerpta de Insidiis* (Berlin, 1905), Fragment 41.

were unwilling to receive a good Monophysite patriarch from a Monophysite emperor: they were not really interested in the theological issue but wanted a patriarch of their own choice. The story certainly shows that the people of Alexandria were jealous of the canonical rights of their church, and resented the interference of the secular authorities: but this hardly proves hostility to the imperial government.

That the Copts welcomed the Persian invaders there is no evidence. They were certainly later remembered as cruel oppressors and persecutors, as appears from a prophecy attributed to Shenuda by a seventh-centuty biography.[33] Nor is there any good evidence that the Copts welcomed the Arabs.[34] The sources are most unreliable and confused, but from the best of them, John, Bishop of Nikiu, who wrote about two generations after the event, it is evident that the rapid subjugation of Egypt by the Arabs was mainly due to the defeatism of Cyrus, the Chalcedonian patriarch and prefect, and to the dynastic disputes which paralysed the government at Constantinople after the death of Heraclius. He records, it is true, that the Arabs were encouraged not only by the weakness of the Roman troops, but by the hostility of the people to Heraclius

[33] M. Amélineau, *Monuments pour servir à l'histoire de l'Egypte chrétienne* (Paris, 1888); cp. *idem, Etude sur le christianisme en Egypte au septième siècle* (Paris, 1887), for a seventh-century Coptic life of Pisentios, Bishop of Coptos, who fled into the desert on the advent of the Persians, and wrote to his flock, "Because of our sins God has abandoned us: he has delivered us to the nations without mercy."

[34] See A. J. Butler, *The Arab Conquest of Egypt* (Oxford, 1903).

on account of the recent persecution.[35] But the reaction of the Egyptians seems to have been confused and uncertain, some fleeing in panic,[36] others deserting to the Arabs,[37] others resisting to the best of their ability.[38] The people of Alexandria were certainly horrified when they learned that they were to be surrendered to the Arabs under the final treaty.[39]

John's own attitude is significant. He regards the Arab conquest not as a deliverance, but as a calamity, the judgment of God upon the emperior Heraclius for persecuting the orthodox. It is to him strictly comparable with the earthquakes and plagues whereby God punished the previous apostasy of Justin and Justinian. But even more significant is the whole tone of John's history. If there had been anything that could truly be called a Coptic national movement, one would have expected it to develop its own version of history, in which the Egyptian people would play a heroic or at least a central role, and its resistance to the alien oppressor would be glorified. John in fact produces a standard history of the Roman Empire, merely reversing the Chalcedonian judgments on the merits of the successive emperors. He denounces [the rulers] Marcion and Pulcheria, Justin and Justinian, and above all Heraclius, the arch-persecutor. But he praises Anastasius, and even Tiberius who was merely tolerant of Monophysitism. He betrays no hatred of the Roman

[35] R. H. Charles, *The Chronicle of John, bishop of Nikiu* (London, 1916), cxv, 9.
[36] *Op. cit.*, cxiii, 6; cxv, 6; cxx, 28.
[37] *Op. cit.*, cxiii, 2; cxix, 1.
[38] *Op. cit.*, cxv, 1-3; 10.
[39] *Op. cit.*, cxx, 24-26.

Empire as such, and so far from rejoicing in its fall, laments the disasters which the apostasy of certain emperors brought upon it.

It remains true, of course, that the Egyptian church almost throughout its history maintained a remarkable solidarity, tenaciously supporting the doctrines of its chiefs, the patriarchs of Alexandria, through thick and thin; provided, of course that these patriarchs were canonically elected and upheld the doctrines of their predecessors. To usurpers, who were intruded by an external authority and betrayed the traditions of the see, it maintained uncompromising resistance. The Egyptian church never wavered in its devotion to the Homoousian doctrine enunciated by Alexander and Athanasius, and the Monophysite doctrine of Dioscorus.

This monolithic solidarity may be attributed to national sentiment, but it is more simply explained by the structure and traditions of the Egyptian church. From the earliest times the bishop of Alexandria had virtually appointed all the other bishops of Egypt, and by tradition he exercised an absolute authority over them. As the Egyptian bishops at Chalcedon protested, when they were ordered to sign the statement of the Dyophysite faith: "The ancient custom has prevailed in the Egyptian diocese that all the bishops obey the archbishop of Alexandria." [40] In these circumstances the Egyptians never heard any view but that of their patriarch, and they naturally accepted it as gospel. That it was the supremacy of the patriarch and not any national spirit of unanimity which produced the solidarity

[40] *Acta Conciliorum Oecumenicorum* II. i. 309.

of the Egyptian church is strongly suggested by the fact that when under Justinian there was for a long period no genuine patriarch in Egypt, the unity of the church broke down and rival parties formed within it.[41]

The people of Egypt—whether they spoke Greek or Coptic—naturally took great pride in the renown of their patriarchal see. The bishops of Alexandria claimed a pre-eminent position in the church and plumed themselves on being unerring champions of orthodoxy. They resented the rival pretentions of the see of Constantinople, and took a certain malicious pleasure in humbling its successive occupants—John Chrysostom, Nestorius, Flavian—whenever they could catch them out in canonical or doctrinal deviations. The people of Egypt rejoiced in their triumphs and were bitterly chagrined at their defeats. The sullen refusal of the Egyptian church to accept any compromise on the Monophysite issue was probably due not so much to the doctrinal differences involved, which were very minute, as to loyalty to Dioscorus' memory. Hence their insistence that Chalcedon, which had condemned him, must be explicitly anathematized; the *Henoticon*,[42] which hedged on this point, was not satisfying to their pride. The Council's recognition of the patriarchal authority and primacy of Constantinople must also have contributed to Egyptian hatred of Chalcedon.

To turn to the Jacobite church of Syria,[43] the picture

[41] See Maspero, *op. cit.*

[42] [This was a document published in 482 by Emperor Zeno which was meant to serve as the basis for the reunion between the Orthodox and the Monophysites.—Ed.]

[43] See R. Devreesse, *La Patriarcat d'Antioche* (Paris, 1945).

of a Syriac-speaking national Monophysite church opposed to a Greek-speaking imperial Orthodox church
does not seem to be true for the period before the Arab
conquest. In the first pace the Monophysite heresy was
in the sixth century by no means confined to Syriac-
speaking areas. John of Ephesus records that John of
Hephaestopolis journeyed throughout Asia Minor, or-
daining priests for the Monophysite congregations, from
Tralles and Ephesus in the west as far as Tarsus, and
also visited Cyprus and Rhodes.[44] The journeys of
James Baradaeus covered not only Syria and Armenia,
but Cappadocia, Cilicia, Isauria, Pamphylia, Lycaonia,
Phrygia, Lycia, Caria, and Asia, as well as Cyprus,
Rhodes, Chios, and Mitylene. Of the twenty-nine sees
to which he consecrated bishops thirteen were in Egypt,
seven in Syria and Mesopotamia, and nine in Asia Minor,
Ephesus, Smyrna, Pergamum, Tralles, Aphrodisias,
Alabanda, Chios, Tarsus, and Seleucia on the Caly-
cadnus.[45] Later John speaks of the spread of the schism
in the Monophysite church from Syria into Armenia,
Cilicia, Isauria, Cappadocia, and Asia.[46] Elsewhere he
describes the flourishing Monophysite churches of
Pamphylia,[47] and he incidentally mentions Monophysite
bishops and communities in cities of Asia Minor: Sardis,
Chalcedon, Nicomedia, Cyzicus, Prusias, Heraclea.[48]

---

[44] John of Ephesus, *Lives of the Eastern Saints*, XXV [Syriac text
and English translation by E. W. Brooks in *Patrologia Orientalis*,
XVIII (1924)].

[45] John of Ephesus, *Lives of the Eastern Saints*, I.

[46] John of Ephesus, *Historiae Ecclesiasticae Fragmenta*, iv. 19; cp.
i. 39 (Cappadocia), ii. 32 (Asia and Cappadocia).

[47] *Op. cit.*, v. 6.

In the second place the heresy did not establish itself in all Syriac-speaking areas. In Syria itself there was, and has been ever since, a strong Chalcedonian church, and in Palestine Monophysitism after initially sweeping the field was soon stamped out. Ernst Stein cites the orthodoxy of Palestine as evidence for the nationalist thesis.[49] Palestine was, he argues, a more Hellenized land than Syria, and such non-Hellenized inhabitants as it had were Jews and Samaritans who stood outside the conflict. This picture is very questionable. The Samaritans were mainly concentrated in the territory of Neapolis, though they spilled over into neighboring cities like Caesarea and Scythopolis.[50] The Jews were dominant in Galilee, where Sepphoris and Tiberias were completely Jewish cities,[51] but seem to have been eradicated from Judea proper after the revolt of Barcochba, and had never been particularly numerous in the coastal plain or beyond the Jordan. Palestine was no more, and probably less, Hellenized than Phoenicia and Syria, and we have evidence of Syriac-speaking Christian townsfolk, who knew no Greek, at Scythopolis[52] and

[48] *Op. cit.*, i. 15 (Sardis), *Lives of the Eastern Saints*, xlvi (Chalcedon, etc).

[49] *Histoire du Bas-Empire*, II, 174 ff.

[50] This may be inferred from the story of the various Samaritan revolts, which were always confined to this area (Malalas, pp. 382-83, 445-47, 487-88 [Bonn Edition]; Procopius, *Aed.* V. VII; *Anecdota* xi. 24-30; Cyril of Scythopolis *Vita Sabae* 70).

[51] Epiphanius *Adversus Haereses* 30. The Jewish revolt under Gallus was apparently in Galilee, its principal stronghold being Sepphoris (Socrates *Historia Ecclesiastica* ii. 33; Sozomen *Historia Ecclesiastica* iv, 7).

[52] Eusebius *Martyrs of Palestine* I. 1.

Gaza,[53] the latter a great center of Hellenic culture.

The Monophysite and Syriac-speaking areas therefore by no means coincided in the sixth century. Monophysitism gradually died in Asia Minor, which remained under the control of an orthodox government, whereas it survived and prospered under the toleration accorded by the Arabs in Syria, though it never ousted orthodoxy there and never penetrated again to Palestine.

Nor until after the Arab conquest was the Syriac language particularly associated with Monophysitism. East of the Euphrates Syriac had a continuous history as a literary language, and here it was used by the churches both orthodox and heretical from the fourth century onwards. In Syria and Palestine Syriac survived only as the spoken language of the lower classes, especially in the country, and Greek was normally used by the churches, though for the benefit of the lower classes some concessions were made to Syriac. At Scythopolis there were at the beginning of the fourth century readers whose duty it was to translate the service into Syriac,[54] and later Publius of Zeugma, when Syriac-speaking postulants sought admission to his Greek-speaking monastery, allowed them to sing the service in their own tongue.[55] The same linguistic division existed in the Monophysite church. Those of its apologists who came from east of the Euphrates, Philoxenus of Hierapolis for instance, and John of Ephesus, wrote in Syriac. Severus of Antioch, who was by origin

[53] Marcus Diaconus *Vita Porphyrii* 66-68; Jerome mentions Syriac-speaking townsfolk at Elusa (*Vita Hilarionis* 25).

[54] See p. 21, n. 52.

[55] Theodoret *Historia Religiosa* 5.

a Pisidian,[56] wrote both his theological works and his letters in Greek, and Zacharias of Mitylene, who came from Gaza,[57] composed his ecclesiastical history and his life of Severus in that language.

There is no evidence that the Monophysites of Syria were politically disaffected to the empire. The only bishop who collaborated with a rebel in these parts was Calandion, the Chalcedonian patriarch of Antioch, who accepted the support of Illus at a time when the legitimate emperor, Zeno, had by the issue of the *Henoticon* proclaimed his sympathy with the Monophysite cause.[58] We possess very long and detailed accounts of the wars waged under Justinian, Justin II, Tiberius, and Maurice between the Persian and the Roman empires in the very areas where Monophysitism was strongest, but there is no hint in them that the Monophysites gave the Persians any aid or comfort, or indeed regarded them with anything but fear and detestation. Nor is there any suggestion in the Monophysite historians that they ever envisaged secession from the empire, or regarded the Romans as alien oppressors. Of the attitude of the Syrian Monophysites in the later Persian wars under Heraclius or during the Arab invasion we have no contemporary evidence.

The case of the Armenians is different. Armenia had been an independent kingdom down to the reign of Theodosius the Great, when it was partitioned between

[56] Zacharias, *Life of Severus*, [in] *Patrologia Orientalis* (Paris), II, i, 10.
[57] *Ibid.*, pp. 23-24.
[58] Evagrius *Historia Ecclesiastica* iii. 16.

Rome and Persia, the latter getting the lion's share. Under alien domination the Armenians continued to feel and act as a nation. They had possessed their own church, which might truly be called national, since the early fourth century. In the middle decades of the fifth century they were involved in a struggle with Persia, which was endeavoring to impose Zoroastrianism on them, and took no part in the councils of Ephesus and Chalcedon. As late as 506 they were unaware of the issues involved, and learned of them only from certain Mesopotamian Monophysites who were being persecuted, at the instigation of the Nestorians, by the Persian government. They naturally accepted the views of their fellow sufferers, and affirmed their unity with the Romans, condemning Nestorius and the council of Chalcedon, and approving "the letter of Zeno blessed emperor of the Romans." When Justin and Justinian reversed Anastasius' ecclesiastical policy, they were apparently not consulted, and did not follow suit. This implied no hostility to Rome, however, for when in 572 they revolted against Persia they appealed to Justin II. He insisted on their subscribing to Chalcedon as a condition of aid, but they soon went back to their old beliefs. Maurice again attempted to impose the Chalcedonian position upon them, but the bishops of Persian Armenia refused to attend his council, and excommunicated the bishops of Roman Armenia, who had conformed. It was thus not hostility to Rome which led the Armenians into heresy; on the contrary they conformed to what was at the time the official Roman position. But having got used to this position they were unwilling to move from it, though they still regarded Rome as their natural ally and protector.[59]

The Arian German tribes are in a way a parallel case. There is, of course, no doubt that the Ostrogoths, Visigoths, Vandals, Burgundians, and Lombards were conscious national or tribal units. The Goths became Arians because they were evangelized at a time when Arianism was the official and dominant doctrine of the eastern part of the Roman Empire, and the other tribes seem to have learned their Christianity from them. The question is why did the German tribes cling so tenaciously to their long outmoded heresy. Was it from national pride or because they believed that it was the true faith? In fact, no doubt they remained Arians from mere conservatism, but they certainly were convinced that Arianism was true and pleasing to God. A remark of Sidonius Apollinaris about the Visigothic king Euric is revealing.[60] Euric was, Sidonius says, a fanatic and persecutor, so much so that "one might be in doubt whether he is leader of his tribe or of his sect." "His mistake is," he goes on, "that he believes that success is granted to him in his dealings and plans in virtue of true religion, whereas he really obtains it in virtue of earthly good fortune." Euric, in other words, like most Christians of his day, believed that God rewarded with worldly success those rulers who held the true faith and stamped out heresy, and attributed his

---

[59] See V. Inglisian, "Chalkedon und die armenische Kirche," in A. Grillmeier and H. Bacht, *Das Konzil von Chalkedon* (Würzburg, 1953), II, 361-417.
[60] Sidonius Apollinaris *Epistula vii. 6. 6.*

own success to his zeal in promoting Arianism and crushing the heresy of the Homoousians.

Of one sect only, so far as I know, has it been claimed that it was at bottom a social movement. Donatism has been represented as a revolutionary uprising of the poor against the rich.[61] For this view there is some solid evidence. Both Augustine and Optatus depict in vivid circumstantial terms the activities of the circumcellions.[62] They gave their protection to tenant farmers against their landlords, to debtors against their creditors, and to slaves against their masters. "No one was allowed to be safe on his estates. The bonds of debtors lost their force, no creditor was free to exact his money at that time." Those who dared to disobey the letters of the Leaders of the Saints suffered dire penalties. Their houses were burnt down, they themselves were forced to work at the mill like slaves, or torn from their carriages and compelled to run behind while their slaves drove.

That circumcellion hands did from time to time exercise such a reign of terror in some areas cannot be doubted. The circumcellions were recruited from the poor peasantry, and were no doubt not averse from paying off old scores against oppressive landlords and extortionate moneylenders when they had a good excuse for doing so in the name of religion. But the circumcellions must be distinguished from the Donatist church;

---

[61] F. Martroye, "Un tentative de revolution sociale en Afrique," *Revue des questions historiques,* LXXVI (1904), 353-416; LXXVII (1905), 1-53.

[62] Augustine *Epistula* 108. 6. 18; 185. 4. 15; Optatus, *op. cit.,* iii. 4.

they were the storm troopers of the movement, whom its official leaders did not always find it easy to control, and some of whose activities they may not have approved.[63] There is, so far as I know, no evidence that the Donatist church ever proclaimed any revolutionary program of community of goods or freeing of slaves or remission of debt. In general, moreover, the activities of the circumcellions were inspired by religious zeal, and their victims were renegades who had deserted to the Catholic fold, or Catholics who had exercised pressure on Donatists to abjure their faith. There is an interesting letter of Augustine to the great senator Pammachius, who owned estates in Numidia, in which he heaps the most fulsome praise upon him for having had the courage to convert his Donatist tenants to catholicism, and expresses the hope that other senatorial landlords will be encouraged to follow his example.[64] From this it would appear that Donatist peasants were generally content to pay their rent to their landlords even if they were Catholics, and that the circumcellions would normally only take action against Catholic landlords if they tried to seduce their tenants from the faith.

The nationalist and socialist theories which I have been discussing seem to me to be based on a radical misapprehension of the mentality of the later Roman Empire. Today religion, or at any rate doctrine, is not with the majority of people a dominant issue and does not arouse major passions. Nationalism and socialism

[63] Augustine *Contra Litteras Petiliani* i. 24. 26; cp. ii. 23. 53, and *Contra Epistulam Parmenianum* i. 11. 17.
[64] Augustine *Epistula* 58.

27

are, on the other hand, powerful forces, which can and do provoke the most intense feelings. Modern historians are retrojecting into the past the sentiments of the present age when they argue that mere religious or doctrinal dissension cannot have generated such violent and enduring animosity as that evinced by the Donatists, Arians, or Monophysites, and that the real moving force behind these movements must have been national or class feeling.

The evidence for nationalism of any kind in the later Roman Empire is tenuous in the extreme. It has been argued that when the imperial government in the fifth century tended to appoint senators of Gallic domicile to posts in Gaul, it was placating a sentiment of "Gaul for the Gauls," which later found expression in the election of Avitus by the Gallic nobility.[65] But these facts imply no more than that Gallic senators expected their share of offices and naturally preferred to serve near home, and that in the anarchy which followed the death of Petronius they saw an opportunity of electing one of themselves to be emperor. Neither Avitus nor his backers had any intention of setting up a Gallic state; he intended to be emperor of the Western empire. No one who has read the letters, poems, speeches, and histories which they wrote can doubt that the literate upper classes of the empire regarded themselves as Romans, as was only natural, seeing that they all shared the same cultural tradition. Of the lower classes we know little, since they were inarticulate. Very many

---

[65] J. Sundwall, *Weströmische Studien* (Berlin, 1915), pp. 8-26.

of them spoke indigenous languages, but if they possessed any national traditions, they have not come down
to us. In their actions, while they rarely displayed any
positive loyalty to the empire, neither did they show
any positive hostility. Usually they accepted Roman
or barbarian with equal apathy.

Nor again, though there was much misery and some
discontent among the lower classes, is there much sign of
a class-conscious hatred of the rich. In times of famine
the urban populace sometimes rioted and lynched un-
popular officials or rich men who were hoarding stocks
of corn, but such outbursts were sporadic and unor-
ganized. Peasant revolts were very rare. The most
notable were those of the Bacaudae in Gaul and later
also in Spain.[66] Three rebellions are known in Gaul,
one under Diocletian, the second under Honorius, and
the third under Valentinian III. All reached formidable
proportions, and required large-scale military opera-
tions to suppress them. They each lasted for a number
of years, were commanded by organized leaders, and
controlled substantial areas—the two last Armorica, that
is, the territory between the English Channel and the
Loire. Unfortunately we have very little information
about their inner character save that the Bacaudae are
characterized as peasants, brigands, and runaway slaves,
and that Exsuperantius, who suppressed the second out-
break in 417, is said to have "restored the laws and
brought back liberty, and not suffered them to be slaves
of their own servants." Here we seem to have some-

[66] The evidence is assembled in "Past and Present," II (1952), 11 ff.

thing more organized than sporadic jacqueries, but these revolts find no parallel in the rest of the empire.

On the other hand there is abundant evidence that interest in theology was intense and widespread. The generality of people firmly believed that not only individual salvation but the fortunes of the empire depended on correct doctrine, and it was natural that they felt passionately on the subject. Not all, of course, were well informed. Many humble Donatists shouted "Deo Laudes" and denounced the Catholics as traditores without any clear understanding of the issues, or at best sang with gusto the songs which Parmenian had composed for their instruction.[67] Many an Egyptian monk could not have explained the subtleties of the Monophysite doctrine and was content to chant "who was crucified for us" after the Trisagion, and to curse the Chalcedonians as Nestorians. But even uneducated people argued theological points with zest, and could cite the key texts and repeat the stock arguments. One need hardly be reminded of Gregory of Nyssa's description of Constantinople during the Arian controversy. "If you ask for your change, the shopkeeper philosophizes to you about the Begotten and the Unbegotten. If you ask the price of a loaf, the answer is 'the Father is greater and the Son inferior;' if you say 'Is my bath

---

[67] Augustine *Epistula* 55. 18. 34; Praedestinatus *de Haeresibus* 43. Other examples of popular songs for the instruction of the ignorant on theological issues are Augustine's *Psalmus contra partem Donati* and Arius' *Thaleia*. If the latter was really, as Athanasius implies (*Orationes contra Arianos* i. 4), sung in the bars of Alexandria, the proletariat of that city must have had a strong taste for theological controversy: the surviving verses (cited in Athanasius *de Synodis* 15) are not very inspiring.

ready?', the attendant declares that the Son is of nothing." [68] And finally thousands of people were prepared to face deportation, pecuniary loss, torture, and even death on theological issues for most of which no national or social undertones can be discovered.

I would contend that under the later Roman Empire most people felt strongly on doctrinal issues and a high proportion had sufficient acquaintance with theology to argue about them with zest if without any deep understanding. It does not, of course, followed that they adopted whatever doctrinal position they held from a rational evaluation of the arguments for and against it. As today and in all ages most people's religious beliefs were determined by a variety of irrational influences. Some were swayed by the authority of a revered theologian, or more often by that of a holy man whose orthodoxy was guaranteed by his austerities and miracles. The great majority accepted what they had been brought up to believe as children, or the dominant belief of their social milieu. Some doctrines made a special appeal to certain classes of society. It has been claimed that in Asia Minor the areas where the rigorist sects prevailed coincided with those where native languages survived. This is not the whole truth, for, as we know from Socrates, there were in Constantinople, Nicomedia, Nicaea, and other great cities cultivated Novatians, like their delightful bishop Sisinnius, who when asked by censorious members of his flock why, being a bishop, he took two baths a day, replied: "Because I have not

[68] Gregory Nyssa, *Oratio de deitate Filii et Spiritus Sancti.*

got time for a third." [69] But the bulk of the more fundamentalist Novatians were Phrygians and Paphlagonians, and Socrates is surely on the right lines when he explains this fact by saying that these people were naturally not addicted to the horse races and the theatre, and regarded fornication with horror.[70] He holds that the austerity of the Phrygians and Paphlagonians is due to the climate—they lie in the zone between the Scythians and Thracians, who are inclined to violent passions, and the peoples of the East, who are subject to their appetites. The truth surely is that they were simple countryfolk, whose life was necessarily somewhat austere, and that they were naturally attracted by a severe doctrine which condemned indulgences to which they were not prone. The fact that they spoke an indigenous language is an index merely of their rusticity, and not of any mysterious affinity between Novatianism and Phrygian national culture.

In brief I would maintain that when the sectaries declared, as they did on our evidence declare: "We hold the true faith and are the true church; our opponents are heretics, and never will we accept their doctrine or communicate with them, or yield to the impious government which supports them," they meant and felt what they said. Why they held their particular beliefs we

---

[69] Socrates [in *Historia Ecclesiastica*] records a number of cultivated Novatian bishops of Constantinople: Marcian (iv. 9), Sisinnius (vi. 22), Chrysanthus (vii. 12), Paul (vii. 17), and also Ablabius, Bishop of Nicaea, a rhetorician (vii. 12). The synod of Pazos, where the rural Novatians adopted the Quartodeciman heresy, was not attended by the leading bishops of the sect, those of Constantinople, Nicaea, Nicomedia, and Cotyaeum (iv. 28).

[70] Socrates *Historia Ecclesiastica* iv. 28.

in many cases cannot divine. Who can tell why in A.D. 450 out of the eight hundred villages in the territory of Cyrrhus one was Arian, one Eunomian, and eight remained stubbornly faithful to the doctrines of Marcion which had been generally condemned for some three centuries? [71] In some cases the sects more or less coincided with social or regional groups, and I have endeavored to explain how this may have come about. But the line of demarcation between orthodoxy and heresy never, except in the case of the Armenians and the Germans, corresponded with anything that can legitimately be called a national, as opposed to a regional, division. It was inhabitants of Egypt, and not Copts, who were Monophysite, and even in Africa, though Donatism made a greater appeal, as a rigorist sect, to the Punic- or Berber-speaking peasantry, many Romanized Africans were found on the Donatist side. And finally the sects never pursued political aims, whether national or social.

[71] Theodoret *Epistula* 81, 113.

For Further Reading

For definition and clarification of technical terms in this study, the reader should consult the following:

CROSS, F. L. (ed.). *The Oxford Dictionary of the Christian Church*. London: Oxford University Press, 1957.

JACKSON, SAMUEL MACAULEY (ed.). *The New Schaff-Herzog Encyclopedia of Religious Knowledge*. Grand Rapids: Baker, 1953.

SMITH, W. and WACE, H. (eds.). *Dictionary of Christian Biography*. 4 vols.; London, 1877-1888.

Concerning heresy and schism:

TURNER, H. E. W. *The Pattern of Christian Truth*. London: Mowbray, 1954.

GREENSLADE, S. L. *Schism in the Early Church*. New York: Harper, 1953.

GRANT, ROBERT. "Nationalism and Internationalism in the Early Church," in the *Anglican Theological Review*, 1959, pp. 167-176.

HARDY, E. R. "The Patriarchate of Alexandria: A Study in National Christianity," in *Church History*, 1946, pp. 81-100.

Facet Books Already Published

Historical Series:

1. *Were Ancient Heresies Disguised Social Movements?* by A. H. M. Jones. 1966
2. *Popular Christianity and the Early Theologians* by H. J. Carpenter. 1966

Social Ethics Series:

1. *Our Calling* by Einar Billing (translated by Conrad Bergendoff). 1965
2. *The World Situation* by Paul Tillich. 1965
3. *Politics as a Vocation* by Max Weber (translated by H. H. Gerth and C. Wright Mills). 1965
4. *Christianity in a Divided Europe* by Hanns Lilje. 1965
5. *The Bible and Social Ethics* by Hendrik Kraemer. 1965
6. *Christ and the New Humanity* by C. H. Dodd. 1965
7. *What Christians Stand For in the Secular World* by William Temple. 1965
8. *Legal Responsibility and Moral Responsibility* by Walter Moberly. 1965
9. *The Divine Command: A New Perspective on Law and Gospel* by Paul Althaus (translated by Franklin Sherman). 1966
10. *The Road to Peace* by John C. Bennett, Kenneth Johnstone, C. F. von Weizsäcker, Michael Wright. 1966

11. *The Idea of a Natural Order: With an Essay on Modern Asceticism*
    by V. A. Demant. 1966
12. *Kerygma, Eschatology, and Social Ethics*
    by Amos Niven Wilder. 1966

Biblical Series:

1. *The Significance of the Bible for the Church*
   by Anders Nygren (translated by Carl Rasmussen). 1963
2. *The Sermon on the Mount*
   by Joachim Jeremias (translated by Norman Perrin). 1963
3. *The Old Testament in the New*
   by C. H. Dodd. 1963
4. *The Literary Impact of the Authorized Version*
   by C. S. Lewis. 1963
5. *The Meaning of Hope*
   by C. F. D. Moule. 1963
6. *Biblical Problems and Biblical Preaching*
   by C. K. Barrett. 1964
7. *The Genesis Accounts of Creation*
   by Claus Westerman (translated by Norman E. Wagner). 1964
8. *The Lord's Prayer*
   by Joachim Jeremias (translated by John Reumann). 1964
9. *Only to the House of Israel? Jesus and the Non-Jews*
   by T. W. Manson. 1964
10. *Jesus and the Wilderness Community at Qumran*
    by Ethelbert Stauffer (translated by Hans Spalteholz). 1964
11. *Corporate Personality in Ancient Israel*
    by H. Wheeler Robinson. 1964
12. *The Sacrifice of Christ*
    by C. F. D. Moule. 1964
13. *The Problem of the Historical Jesus*
    by Joachim Jeremias (translated by Norman Perrin). 1964

Body, 11 on 14 Janson
Display, Garamond
Paper: White Spring Grove E.F.

brief, brilliant treatments of vital aspects of faith *
and life by leading authorities in the church today

DATE DUE			
3/3/28			
GAYLORD			PRINTED IN U.S.A.

FORTRESS PRESS
PHILADELPHIA, PA. 19129

75c